Warren Buffett

A Biography

Patrick Evans

Table of Contents

INTRODUCTION

This book is an exploration of the life of one of the finest investment minds of the 21st century and how he built a formidable business empire.

Fondly called the "Wizard of Omaha," Warren Edward Buffett is as great an investor as they come.

Born into the family of Howard and Leila Buffett, in the largest city of Nebraska, United States of America, he sits on one of the largest financial war chest anywhere in the world – Berkshire Hathaway.

The chairman of one of America's foremost multinational conglomerate holding company, Buffett has a personal net worth of $87 billion. The company is worth over $600 billion.

The son of a stockbroker and former congressman, Buffett's wealth is only second to those of two other men in the entire world. With a good education and an incredible understanding of modern investing in his arsenal, his capacity for wealth creation is only rivaled by his passion for philanthropy. He has committed to giving away 99% of his fortune to charitable causes.

Buffett's journey to staggering wealth started in his tender years. He started investing in stocks at the tender age of 11. Prior to that, he had tried his hands out on petty trading selling Coca-Cola, chewing gum and what other items he found profitable. He also worked at his grandfather's grocery store.

His pinball machine leasing business which he started in high school was so successful that he sold it for $1,200.

Buffett graduated from the University of Nebraska at 19 after attending the Wharton School of the University of Pennsylvania for a period of two years. Graduate school was in Columbia Business School where he met the legendary Benjamin Graham who became his mentor and opened his eyes to the new world of value investing. His last academic stop was at the New York Institute of Finance.

Following two brief stints working with his father and Benjamin Graham, Buffett started investing through his partnerships. He found a brilliant and trusted partner in

Charlie Munger and needless to say, their friendship and business collaboration has been mutually rewarding.

After recording impressive returns on his investments through the Buffett Partnership Ltd., Warren liquidated the partnership and shifted his focus to building Berkshire Hathaway into a formidable diversified holding company.

From a struggling textile company, Warren Buffett has built Berkshire into a multinational conglomerate with a highly diversified business portfolio. The company is a force to be reckoned with in industries like confectionary, jewelry sales, retail, railroads, encyclopedias, home furnishing, newspaper publishing, electric and gas utilities among others.

While Berkshire holds full ownership of companies like GEICO, Duracell, BNSF Railway, Fruit of The Loom and a host of others; it holds minority but valuable stakes in The Coca-Cola Company, Wells Fargo, American Express, Bank of America and Apple Inc.

Under the leadership of Warren Buffett, the company has maintained a 19.0% average in the annual growth of its share value beating the market average year in year out.

Every year in his home town of Omaha, Nebraska, Buffett hosts one of the most anticipated investment events in the world – Berkshire Hathaway shareholders meeting. The event registers thousands in attendance from around the world, all present to glean nuggets of wisdom from the investment sage.

Warren Buffett is not all about business only. Once married to Susan Thompson. The couple had 3 children – Susie, Howard and Peter Buffett. Susan passed on in July 2004. Before then, Susan and Warren had been living separately. Buffett married Astrid Menks in 2006, on the occasion of his 76th birthday. Astrid was 60 at the time and had lived with Buffett since Susan's departure to San Francisco in 1977.

Buffett's philanthropic efforts are remarkable. He has pledged to donate a large chunk of his wealth to charitable causes through the Bill and Melinda Gates Foundation. Following many charitable acts including the auction of his 2001 Lincoln Town Car to raise money for Girls, Inc. and a luncheon with himself to raise millions for Glide Foundation, Warren Buffet alongside Bill Gates and Mark Zuckerberg signed a promise called the "Gates – Buffett Giving Pledge." They made a commitment to give away half of their wealth to charity and invite other wealthy people to do the same. In 2018, Buffett made a donation of $3.4 billion.

In addition to being a philanthropic capitalist, Buffett regularly lends his voice and resources to political and social causes. He endorsed and made financial contributions to Barrack Obama's presidential campaign in 2008. Barrack Obama once identified Buffett as a potential economic advisor and Secretary of the U.S Treasury. In 2003, Buffett played the role of financial advisor to Arnold Schwarzenegger during his election campaign. He also endorsed Hilary Clinton's presidential bid in December 2015.

Buffett has expressed his opinion on various government policies and programmes, particularly on health care. His view is that government spending on health care is a far cry from what it should. Warren says that health care cost should account for 13 to 14% of GDP. He has commented on issues like taxes, America's trade deficit, dollar and gold, renewable energy and many more.

Warren Buffett continues to live in his home in Omaha from where he is influencing the whole wide world.

Chapter 1

Early Life

The place was Omaha, Nebraska. The year was 1930. And the child was Warren Edward Buffett.

Born into the family of Leilah and Howard Buffett, he was the second of three children – the only son. His sisters are Dorris and Roberta Buffett.

Buffett's father was a stockbroker, investor, and politician. He represented Nebraska's second congressional district in the U.S House of Representatives serving four terms between 1942 and 1952.

Buffett's formal education began at Rose Hill Elementary School. He went on to attend Alice Deal Junior High School when his father's political career took the family to Washington D.C. He spent the rest of his high school days in Woodrow Wilson High School and graduated in 1947. The caption on his yearbook picture could not be apter. It read, "likes math; a future stock broker."

Buffett was a smart kid with an amazing aptitude for numbers, money, and business. He left acquaintances dazed with his ability to easily calculate columns of numbers off the top of his head. Till this present day, Buffett still leaves business colleagues amazed with each display of his numerical ability. His incredible love for statistics spurred him to make smart bets on horse races. He once created tip sheets at his local race track.

He has also been a voracious reader from his early years. At age 11, he had read through every book on investment in the Omaha Public Library and his father's office.

Buffett was an early starter in the world of business and investment. Some would say he inherited his initial financial instincts from his father. His entrepreneurial enthusiasm was further stirred by a book he read at the age of seven, *One Thousand Ways to Make $1000*. This was the book that taught him the value of compound interest.

He started his first business at age 6 selling packs of Coca-Cola. He made a five cent profit on every bottle sold by selling each for a nickel having bought six packs from his grandfather's grocery store at twenty-five cents. Buffett soon added chewing gum and lemonade to his inventory.

As a child, his interest in the stock market was nurtured in a regional stock brokerage not far from his father's office where he spent a lot of time. He visited the New York Stock Exchange at the age of ten while on a trip to New York City.

Aged 11, young Buffett made his first foray into the investment world. He bought six shares – 3 for himself and 3 for his sister, Dorris - at Citi Service, an oil and gas company. Soon after his purchase, the share price fell below $28 per share from $38. But Buffett was not one to chicken out at the first scare. The price later took a rebound and Buffett sold at $40. In addition to his profit, he also learned the value of patience in the investment game as the shares eventually shot up to $200.

His entrepreneurial pursuits continued through high school. His first job was as a paperboy, delivering newspapers from door to door. He went around selling stamps, golf balls, magazine, etc. At the age of 15, teenage Buffett had a monthly income of $175 from delivering *Washington Post* newspapers.

Warren later worked as an editor at *Stable – Boy Selections*, a horse racing tip sheet. Together with a high school friend,

Don Danly, he started a pinball leasing business. They had purchased a used pinball machine at $25 and placed it in a local barbershop. Shortly after, they scaled the business by acquiring several pinball machines placed in different barber shops across Omaha. His weekly earning on the business was as high as $50. They eventually sold the business to a war veteran for $1,200.

Buffett cultivated the habit of saving and investing quite early. As a teenager, he saved and invested a good lot of the money he made from his business ventures. 15-year-old Buffett had $2,000 in savings. He bought a 40-acre farmland in Nebraska and employed a farm laborer to work on it. Warren would later support himself in college with the profit realized from the land.

Buffett's childhood entrepreneurial ventures would prove instrumental to his future business engagement has he had developed an unrelenting work ethic and such resourcefulness that his peers could only envy.

Chapter 2

Warren
and Benjamin Graham

When Warren Buffett graduated from High School in 1947, proceeding to college was the least of his desires. He had achieved some success in business and investment, and he was ready to go bigger. He, however, succumbed to pressure from his father and enrolled at the University of Pennsylvania's Wharton School of Business and Finance. He was only at Wharton for two years in which period he joined the Alpha Sigma Phi fraternity.

Warren transferred to the University of Nebraska – Lincoln after returning home to Omaha following his father's defeat in the 1948 Congressional race. He successfully combined studying with working full-time, graduating in 3 years with a Bachelor of Science in Business Administration.

After obtaining his degree, Buffett was ready to call it quits with formal education. But he was again urged to apply to Harvard Business School. He applied, but Harvard deemed him too young and rejected his application. He was 19 at the time. Looking back, one can hardly think of a worse admission decision on Harvard's part. Warren then learned that Benjamin Graham taught at Columbia Business School. He enrolled for a Master's in Economics and graduated in 1951. It was at Columbia Business School that he had the rare privilege of learning from the iconic value investor, Benjamin Graham. Graham became Buffett's mentor teaching him the profound principles of value investing.

A British-born American, Benjamin Graham was an investor, economist, and professor. He is regarded as the "father of value investing." His legendary works in the field of neoclassical investing are well encapsulated in two texts – *Security Analysis* (1934) with David Dodd and *The Intelligent Investor* (1949). Warren Buffett once described the book, *The Intelligent Investor*, as "the greatest book on investing ever written."

Graham, alongside David Dodd, pioneered the teaching of the principles of value investing in Columbia Business School, an investment philosophy that would go on to revolutionize the way value is perceived and determined in the stock market.

Value investing as an investment paradigm involves the acquisition of securities at a price lower than their intrinsic value based on some fundamental analysis. Concepts like buy-and-hold investing, fundamental analysis, buying within the margin of safety, minimal debt, activist investing, investor psychology and concentrated diversification form the constituent component of the idea of value investing. Its goal is to determine the intrinsic value of a company and make investment decisions accordingly.

Graham did more than write about intelligent investing; he was indeed an intelligent investor. His approach was to buy stocks that were almost devoid of risk at a very low price and milk them in the long term for maximum profit.

One of his stand-out calls was on the stock of a transportation company run by the Rockefellers, Northern Pipe Line. The company had bond holdings worth $95 per share, and its stock was trading at $65 a share. Graham tried to persuade the management to sell the company's bond holdings, but they declined. Not long thereafter, he became a member of the Board of Directors and influenced the company to sell its bond and pay a dividend to the tune of $70 per share.

Though simple, the principles taught by Graham were profound, practicable and, of course, profitable. It did not take long before the 21-year-old Warren Buffett became a devoted disciple of this investment philosophy and a favorite protégé of Benjamin Graham. A high-flyer in graduate school, Buffett was the only student to make an A+ in one of Graham's classes.

Graham was more than Buffett's mentor, he was his hero. Buffett's investment strategy and philosophy were inspired by the principles grasped from Graham's book, *The Intelligent Investor*, which he read a dozen and a half times.

On a memorable Saturday in 1951, 20 year old Buffett visited the Columbian library. He was reading an old edition of *Who's Who* when he learned that Graham was the chairman of Government Employees Insurance Company (GEICO). A week later, he dashed out to Washington D.C where the headquarters of GEICO was located.

On arriving in Washington, he headed straight for GEICO's office. It was a Saturday, and this was 1951, so the doors were locked when he arrived. But Buffett was not about to give up so easily. He pounded on the door relentlessly until a janitor showed up to let him in.

Buffett was on a fact-finding mission but it was not a working day, so there was nobody in the office to speak to except the janitor and one man – Lorimer Davidson. Warren introduced himself as a student of Graham and the conversation that ensued lasted over four hours. Buffett had loads of questions about insurance, the company, and its business practices and Davidson had the answers to his questions. He was the Financial Vice President of the organization and would later become its CEO. Buffett had this to say about his encounter with Lorimer Davidson, "He answered my questions, taught me the insurance business and explained to me the competitive advantage that GEICO had." He added, "That experience changed my life." Buffett would later acquire GEICO entirely through Berkshire Hathaway.

Buffett's academic pursuit did not stop at Columbia Business School. He went further to study at the New York Institute of Finance. He had a goal. He was headed for Wall Street.

But Wall Street was not to be. The two most influential people in his life – his father and Benjamin Graham – advised him against it. Buffett then offered to work for Graham partnership without pay, but Graham turned down the offer. He would rather hire Jews who would not be employed by Gentile firms at the time.

Buffett returned home to Omaha and took a job at his father's brokerage firm. To conquer his fear of public speaking, Buffett enrolled for a Dale Carnegie public speaking course. With his newly acquired public speaking skill, he was bold enough to take a job teaching Investment Principles at a night class at the University of Nebraska – Omaha.

In this period, Warren invested majorly in a Texaco station and some real estate, neither of which was successful. It was about this time that he started seeing Susan Thompson. Things moved quickly between them and in April of 1952, they were married at the Dundee Presbyterian Church. They moved into a 3-bedroom apartment that cost $65 a month. It was a humble abode where they had a family of mice for company. They soon welcomed Susie, their first-born daughter into the home. Money was tight, so baby Susie's bed had to be made in a dresser drawer.

Things had to change, and they had to change fast. It started in 1954 with a call from Benjamin Graham. Graham offered Buffett an opportunity to work for him, and Buffett gladly accepted the offer. He started Buffett off with an annual paycheck of $12,000. Buffett moved his family to the suburbs of New York.

His job was to look for investment opportunities that Graham partnership could cash in on. The bulk of his time was spent analyzing S&P reports to find such investment opportunities.

The Buffetts welcomed their second child, Howard Graham Buffett, into the world in April 1954.

A tough boss, Graham's philosophy and approach to value investing was number driven. He did not concern himself with issues like the capacity of management or corporate leadership when investing. He simply looked at the price of the stock in relation to its intrinsic value to determine the profitability of the investment.

Buffett had a slightly divergent approach. He was interested in the internal workings of a company and its strategy for gaining or maintaining a competitive advantage. The differences in their philosophies had begun to emerge.

Benjamin Graham called it a day with his partnership in 1956. He retired and dissolved the partnership.

With his personal saving well over $174,000, Buffett returned to Omaha and was ready to start something of his own.

On May 1, 1956, Buffett hit the ground running with seven limited partners including his sister Doris and Aunt Alice, with a capital of $105,000. With a personal stake of $100, the Buffett Associates Ltd was born. The portfolio was worth around $300,000 before the end of the year. It was only the beginning; He had bigger plans.

He purchased a 5-bedroom stucco house for $31,500. He had his office in one of its bedrooms where he managed his partnerships. He nicknamed the house "Buffett's Folly" and lives there till this present day. He later moved his office out of his house to a proper office in town.

Within a period of five years, Warren's partnerships were generating an outstanding 251.0% profit. In the same period, the Dow could only manage 74.3%. Buffett became famous in his town. He was hounded for stock tips by every Tom, Dick, and Harry. He did not give any.

35% of the partnership's capital was invested in Sanborn Map Company. The shrewd investor that he is, Buffett explained that while the investment portfolio of the company was worth $65 per share, its stock had traded for only $45 per share. There was a value gap of $20. Buffett went all in as an activist investor, purchasing 23% of the company's outstanding shares. His stake in the company got him a seat on the board. Forming an alliance with other dissatisfied shareholders, Buffett and his allies had 44% of the company's shares under their belt. The board was keen on avoiding a proxy contest, so it offered to buy back shares at a fair valuation. The company successfully repurchased 77% of outstanding shares giving Warren Buffett a 50 percent return within 24 months.

In 1962, Warren Buffett met his partner, Charles Thomas Munger. Charlie Munger, as he is fondly called, was born in Omaha, Nebraska and had, in fact, worked as a teenager at Buffett & Son, a grocery store owned by Buffett's grandfather. He had just returned from California. Munger was a Harvard trained lawyer and had considerable experience in investing.

Introduced by a mutual friend, Buffett and Munger immediately became inseparable both as friends and business partners. Munger today serves as the vice chairman of Berkshire Hathaway, playing the role of Buffett's right-hand man.

Chapter 3

Berkshire Hathaway

I n 1962, Buffett's multiple partnerships had exceeded $7.2 million in value, of which over $1million was Buffett's personal stake. He was a millionaire.

Instead of charging a fee for the partnerships, he took one-quarter of the profits above 4 percent. In a smart move, he merged the partnerships into a single entity known as Buffett Partnership Ltd. and raised the minimum investment to $100,000. The office of the company was on Farnan Street, Kiewit Plaza, Omaha.

On December 12, 1962, Buffett started acquiring shares in a textile manufacturing firm, Berkshire Hathaway, for $7.50 per share. The company was managed by Seabury Stanton who was its President. Its emergence, however, dates back to 1955 when a merger took place between two cotton mills,

Berkshire Fine Spinning Associates and Hathaway Manufacturing Company.

Berkshire as a textile company was struggling at the time. Warren had noticed a positive growth pattern in the price trajectory of the company's stock whenever it shut down a mill and was convinced that the company was selling its stock at a discount to its actual value.

In 1964, the management of Berkshire offered to buy Buffet's shares for $11.50. He was open to the idea of selling until he received the written tender offer of $11.375 per share. Displeased with the management's failure to honor the original deal, he decided to seize control of the company and started acquiring more of its stock for this purpose.

On May 10, 1965, after acquiring 49% of the company's stock, Buffett named himself Director. He had to salvage the company from its precarious state owing to terrible management in previous years. He immediately fired Stanton and appointed Ken Chase president of the company and gave him complete autonomy in managing its affairs.

Instead of giving Ken stock options which Buffett thought would be unfair on shareholders; he ensured his new president got a loan of $18,000 for the acquisition of 1,000 shares of the company's stock.

In 1966, Buffett decided to close the partnership to new money. In his letter, he wrote: *"...unless it appears that circumstances have changed (under some conditions, added capital will improve result) or unless new partners can bring some asset to the partnership other than simply capital, I intend to admit no additional partners to BPL."*

In 1976, two years after Warren became a director in Berkshire Hathaway, he invited Jack Ringwalt to his office. Jack Ringwalt was the founder and controlling shareholder in National Indemnity, an insurance company. Buffett wanted to know how much the company was worth and Ringwalt's reply was at least $50 per share. Though the company's share was trading at $33, Ringwalt had included a $17 premium to arrive at $50.

Warren made an offer to buy the company for $8.6 million right away. Ringwalt accepted, and the deal was done. In the same year, Berkshire paid a dividend of 10 cents per share on its outstanding stock. Berkshire has never again paid a dividend since then. According to Warren, "He must have been in the bathroom when the dividend was declared."

In May 1969, just after what had been his most successful year as an investor, Buffett decided to liquidate the partnership and distribute its assets among the partners. His reason was that he was "unable to find any bargains in the current market." He spent the better part of the year liquidating the entire portfolio excluding only two – Berkshire and Diversified Retailing.

After distributing the shares of Berkshire among the partners, Buffett, by a letter, informed them that he remains a stakeholder in the company but disclaimed any future obligation to the partners. He held 29% of Berkshire stock at the time.

Buffett became the Chairman of the Board of Berkshire Hathaway in 1970. He wrote his first letter to shareholders in the same year, a tradition he has kept over the years. He finally had control, and his astuteness in capital allocation was soon recognized by all.

His growing wealth notwithstanding, Buffett led a frugal lifestyle on his salary of $50,000 annually.

The profit from textile began to dwindle till it reached a miserable $45,000 while insurance and banking raked in $2.1 and $2.6 million respectively. Buffett knew it was time to reposition Berkshire Hathaway.

An opportunity came knocking. Buffett was offered the opportunity to buy See's Candy. See's Candy made chocolates and sold them at a premium relative to the prices charged by other chocolate brands. See's Candy was a profitable company, and its balance sheet reflected that fact. Buffett valued the company at $25 million and was willing to dole out cash to purchase it. The owners of the company thought otherwise; they held out for $30 million. But Buffett was not going to shift grounds. He closed the deal at $25 million. It was Berkshire's most expensive acquisition at the time.

Berkshire was on an acquisition spree, and only a few industries were immune to its overreaching arm. The company started acquiring stock in the Washington Post Company in 1973. Buffett joined the board as he became friends with Katherine Graham who was in charge of the company and its flagship newspaper.

In 1976, Buffett re-established his relationship with GEICO, only this time as an investor. The company had recently recorded huge losses, and the value of its stock had plunged to as low as a miserable $2 per share. Warren quickly identified the problem of the company as incompetent management and thought all was not lost as the very business of the company was still intact.

Over the next few years, Berkshire transformed the fortunes of GEICO. It grew its stake in the company significantly and seized control of its management. GEICO eventually became a wholly owned subsidiary of Berkshire. The company emerged once again as an insurance giant and Berkshire reaped millions in returns.

Berkshire went on to acquire Wesco Financial, another company in the insurance sector. The acquisition portending a possible conflict of interest got the attention of the SEC. An investigation was conducted by the SEC, but no charges were leveled.

The expansionary drive continued with Berkshire parting with $32.5 million to buy the Buffalo Evening News. The acquisition attracted anti-trust charges instigated by Buffalo Courier Express. At the end of the tussle in 1982, only one company was standing, and it was not Buffalo Courier Express.

In 1983, Berkshire made another exciting acquisition. The company was Furniture Mart located in Nebraska. Built from the ground up by Rose Blumpkin, a Russian-born immigrant, the company was a multi-million dollar furniture retailer. In a deal that was wrapped up in one short conversation, Buffett asked Rose if she was interested in selling the company and she immediately answered in the affirmative, naming a $60 million price. With a handshake and a signed one-page agreement, the deal was done.

Berkshire soon took an interest in S&F, maker of Kirby vacuum cleaners and World Book encyclopedia. With existing share ownership of about 250,000, Buffett intimated the company's management of his desire to consummate a merger. The company gladly accepted. S&F was a dollar cash generating powerhouse, and Berkshire had it in its portfolio within a week. Berkshire's share price took a jump from $2,600 to a peak of $80,000 in the 1990s.

In a most ironic corporate tale, Capital Cities purchased ABC for $3.5 billion on March 18, 1985. The media industry was taken aback as ABC was four times the size of Capital Cities at the time. Berkshire was not missing in action. It had previously started acquiring stock in ABC in 1979 and in exchange for his role in helping to finance the acquisition by Capital Cities; Warren was able to secure a 25% stake in the new company, Capital Cities/ABC.

In 1987, Berkshire became the largest shareholder in Salomon Inc., an investment bank, after purchasing a 12%

stake in the company. Buffett became a director of the company. A scandal later broke out in Salomon Inc. involving its CEO John Gutfreund. This paved the way for Buffett to become chairman of the company and was able to quell the storm that threatened to upturn the company's boat by rooting out the prior corporate culture.

In one of Berkshire's most profitable investment, Buffett started purchasing The Coca–Cola Company stock, buying as much as 7% of the company for $1.02 billion. In three short years, Berkshire's Coca–Cola stock was worth more than the entire value of Berkshire when he made the investment.

The stories of Berkshire's expansionary acquisitions are endless. The company is a behemoth with holdings in industries like confectionary, jewelry sales, retail, railroads, real estate, encyclopedias, home furnishing, newspaper publishing, electric and gas utilities among others.

With a highly diversified portfolio, there are only a handful of industries where Berkshire does not play today.

In the rail transport industry, Berkshire wholly owns and controls the second largest freight line in North America, BNSF Railway.

As far as men's apparel goes, the company's subsidiary, Fruit of Loom Inc. is the biggest retailer of men's underwear in the entire country.

The company is well represented in the leading sectors across America. Its portfolio includes Clayton Homes in the modular houses sector, McLane Co., Inc. in trucking; RC Willey Homes Furnishings in the furniture space; NetJets in the jet rental business to mention a few.

In the jewelry industry alone, Borsheim's Fine Jewelry, Helzberg Diamonds, and Ben Bridge Jeweler Inc. are all subsidiaries of Berkshire.

The company has huge stakes in many Fortune 500 companies including Apple Inc. and American Express Co.

It equally retains large holdings in a number of top US airline carriers. The mix comprises Southwest Airlines, American Airlines, Delta Airlines, and United Airlines.

With a market capitalization of over US$496 billion in 2018, Berkshire Hathaway is the third largest public company in the world and seventh largest company in the S&P 500 Index.

The geometric growth in the stock price of Berkshire is absolutely incredible. From $275 in 1980 to $32, 500 in 1995 and well over $308,530 in November 2018, Berkshire is a league of its own. On February 1, 2019, Berkshire's class A shares sold for $313, 350.00 becoming the most expensive shares on the New York Stock Exchange. Berkshire owes this fact to its refusal to split its stock and its decision not to pay dividend aside from the one time it actually did.

Buffett has built an empire, and it's the first of its kind.

Chapter 4

The Best and Worst Investment Decisions Made By Warren Buffett

ᴥᴥᴥᴥᴥᴥᴥᴥᴥᴥᴥᴥᴥᴥᴥᴥᴥ

Warren Buffett currently has a net worth of $83.1 billion. This effectively makes him the third wealthiest person in the world. The biggest part of his wealth is from the shares in his company, Berkshire Hathaway.

He is also regarded as one of the most successful investors in the world. He has single-handedly transformed underperforming companies into million dollar investments.

Over the course of 55 years, Berkshire has expanded from a textile manufacturing company into a conglomerate. The company has investments in industries such as insurance, food, banking, investment, etc.

Buffett did not stumble into being a billionaire; it was through years of hard work and persistence. He had the ability to recognize opportunities and to cash in on them. This was because of the influence of his mentor, Benjamin Graham, and his friend, Charlie Munger.

Graham was Buffett's teacher, inculcating the discipline of value investing into him. However, it was Charles Munger who helped him diversify his investment beyond Graham's teachings.

Over the years, both men have managed to amass wealth by making intelligent investments. Some of the times, they had no idea of the rewards that would follow their decisions.

Warren Buffett's Biggest Investments

Buffett's investment journey began in 1962 when he first invested in a textile company located called Berkshire Hathaway. He subsequently bought some of their shares.

In 1965, he began aggressively buying shares in the company. This was after he was convinced that the company needed new leadership. Ironically, several years later, Buffett would announce that his buying of Berkshire Hathaway was one of his biggest mistakes.

He further diversified into owning insurance companies. This was because he understood that there was a huge return to being made in that field. Principally, clients pay premiums today to possibly receive payments decades later.

Buffett realized how this could work in his favor and latched on to it. He used Berkshire Hathaway as a holding company to purchase the National Indemnity Company. This became the first of many insurance companies he would purchase over the course of decades.

Apart from the initial investment in Berkshire Hathaway, other extraordinary investment decisions by Buffett abound. They include:

Investment with Goldman Sachs

After the financial crisis of the 2000s, a lot of investors were skeptical about putting money into new businesses. However, that was not the case with Warren Buffett.

He decided to invest $5 billion into **Goldman Sachs**, an investment company. This step has become known as Buffett's 'bet on brains.'

Warren Buffett received $5 billion in Goldman Sachs preferred stock. Goldman eventually ended up buying back the preferred stock for $5.64 million. This was in 2011 when

Goldman Sachs received Federal Reserve's approval to buy back the shares.

Initially, Buffett was reluctant to give up the shares. This was because at that time the shares were averaging $1.4 million in dividends every day.

Another of his smartest investments is his investment in **Coca-Cola**. Buffett started buying Coca-Cola shares in 1988. Eventually, he was able to purchase up to 7% of the company's stock for $1.02 billion.

This move would turn out to be one of his best deals for Berkshire Hathaway. More than 30 years after he purchased the shares, they are up by 1,350%. This also does not include the dividends Berkshire has received from Coca-Cola over the past three years.

In fact, currently, Coca-Cola pays Berkshire Hathaway $592 million per year. Much of the success of the Coca-Cola deal is hinged on Buffett's refusal to sell the company's shares.

Going further, another investment that has yielded huge returns is **Buffett's investment in See's Candies**. This has yielded huge returns in investment even though it is just a little part of Berkshire Hathaway's operations.

With a little over $25 million, Buffett has made over $1.35 billion for his investors. Even though Berkshire Hathaway has invested $32 million into the business over the years, it was still a lucrative deal.

In 2011 when Buffett set out to purchase **Bank of America's shares**, he was taken to be making a huge mistake. He purchased $5 billion of the company's preferred stock with a 6% dividend. He also further negotiated the right to buy the company's shares at a future date.

The arrangement was that his company would have the right to purchase the bank's shares anytime before September 2021. The price was set at just $7-14 per share. This move seemed ludicrous because, at that time, the bank's stock was literally worthless. The warranty he got for future transactions was even less than the worth of the stocks at that time.

However, six years later, in 2017, the price of the bank's shares has all but tripled. The investment resulted in a gain of more than $14.2 million for Buffett. Also, Bank of America's dividend has also increased to even more than what Berkshire Hathaway was receiving from its preferred shares.

Following this, Buffett made another smart move. He exchanged his warrant for 700 million shares of the bank. This move made him the bank's largest shareholder.

Part of Buffett's wizardry is in knowing when to sell off his shares to get the best returns. Commenting on this, he stated that like everyone else, the challenge of selling at the right time affects him too.

Going further, he stated that it would be easy if one had the ability to look through an always clean rear-view mirror. Unfortunately, he agreed, the glass is fogged and unclear.

However, that notwithstanding, Buffett has shown an uncanny ability to sell his shares at the most profitable times. One example of such is his investment in mortgage agency Freddie Mac. The precision with which he sold his stock in the government-backed company made it seem like he was an oracle.

Buffett first bought the shares in 1988, the same year he bought the Coca-Cola shares. The shares were bought for $4 per share.

Over the years, he enjoyed a return of over 1,500% as the stock soared to an all-time high of $70 per share. However,

Buffett slowly began selling all of his Freddie Mac shares. By 2000, he had sold virtually all of his stake in the company.

Buffett stated his reason was that he noticed that the company was taking unnecessary risks. He noted that the company was putting its growth at risk because they were so focused on making returns.

It turned out that he was right to tow that path. At the moment, Freddie Mac traded for less than $3. This was less than the original sum Buffett paid for one share over 30 years ago.

Apart from these, Buffett has made a lot of other bets on companies that eventually paid off. One of such is his railroad deal. When Berkshire acquired Burlington Northern Santa Fe Railroad in 2009, it was their biggest acquisition.

Prior to that time, Berkshire already owned nearly 25% of the company. Altogether, Buffett had to pay a whopping $36 billion for the railroad. Even Buffett admitted that the deal was really expensive.

However, the cost notwithstanding, there is no doubt he made the right call. The current estimate of BNSF's current value is put anywhere between 91 to 93 billion dollars.

Finally, Buffett has proven time and again that he is perhaps the smartest businessman alive. He has always been a firm believer that simple low-cost index funds are the smartest way people should invest.

Of course, he also has a habit of putting his money where his mouth is. He wagered $500,000 of his own money on the deal. He stated that an S&P fund would beat a slew of funds selected by hedge fund manager Ted Seides.

After a period of nine years, the difference was startling. The total return for the S&P index fund had an 85.4% turnover rate over the 22% generated by the hedge funds. In fact, Ted Seides, in a bid to save face, conceded the bet early.

Warren Buffett's Worst Investments

People often make the mistake of assuming that Buffett has not made any bad investment decisions. This is perhaps by the pile of success stories he has. Nothing could be further from the truth.

As a matter of fact, Buffett considers his purchase of a majority stake in Berkshire Hathaway a bad investment decision. This is surprising considering that it was that platform that he was launched from. In fact, currently, the "A' rated shares of the company are valued at over $280,000.

When Buffett acquired Berkshire, the company was struggling. He had made the assumption that he would hit the jackpot when other mills shut down. Based on this assumption, he bought a lot of stocks.

However, the company later attempted pushing him out. In spite of this, he bought the entire company, fired the leadership and stayed on for twenty more years. He ended up regretting that move.

Buffett believes that would have made more money if the time and money invested in the business was moved elsewhere. He believes if the funds had been sunk into buying insurance companies, he would make an extra $200 billion.

The mistake with Berkshire Hathaway is one of the few mistakes the businessman made over the course of his career. There are several others which include:

The purchase of Waumbec Textile Company

One would think that after realizing his mistake purchasing a textile company that the mistake would not be repeated. Wrong. Just 13 years after the purchase of Berkshire Hathaway, Warren Buffett bought another textile company called Waumbec Mills.

Buffett would later admit his error in buying the mill. In 1975, two years after purchase, the mill was shut down.

Making Investments into Tesco

In 2012, Berkshire had ownership of 415 million shares of the company, Tesco. However, mysteriously, Buffett decided to sell some of the shares. However, Berkshire remained deeply invested.

Two years later, Tesco crumpled. It was revealed that they had overstated their profits and this led to the tumbling of the company's shares. It was then that Buffett announced that he had had concerns about Tesco's management. And that it had been the reason he sold their stocks in the first place, netting them a profit of $43 million.

He did not go through with the sale of the remaining stocks. That delay cost Berkshire $444 million after-tax loss.

Failing to invest in Google

At the moment, Warren Buffett's impressive portfolio does not boast of even one Google stock. He has stated that this is something he regrets.

In 2017, during a general meeting of investors, he informed them of this regret. He stated that he made a mistake by not purchasing shares in the tech giant when he had the opportunity.

In his defense, he stated that his hesitance had been because he did not fully understand the business model they used. He stated that it was not an excuse. He should have found a way to figure them out, especially as he was already a client of the Google ad business.

Purchasing the United State's Airways stock

Although the US Airways stock is not included in failed Buffett's stock, he did regret the purchase of the stocks. He made the purchase of $358 million worth of shares in 1989.

After the purchase of the stocks, their values never appreciated. Forbes later on reported that in the end, Buffett got his principal and dividends back. However, he did not make any profit from the venture.

This was particularly painful for the businessman as he had never bought stocks without amassing profit. The lesson to be learned from the experience is that research is very crucial when embarking in any investment. This is true whether you are a beginner or an experienced investor.

Deciding Not To Buy Amazon Stock

In a 2017 interview session, Buffett was asked why he never invested in Amazon. He stated that he hadn't an answer.

Expressing his regret, he revealed that he contemplated purchasing stocks from the company for a long time. He stated that he admired it for a long time. However, just like in the case with Google, he stated that he had no understanding of the model at that time.

Warren Buffett has the philosophy of not buying into businesses he did not fully understand. Understandably, that is a wise stance. On the flipside also, it may be unwise not to take risks with new startups or unfamiliar terrains. Partnering with others could be a way of solving the problem.

Failing To Do Purchase on The Dallas-Fort Worth NBC Station

This happens to be one of the few instances where Buffett's loss did not come from flopping of shares.

The shares had initially been offered to him for the price of $35 million. Buffett turned down the offer. This was even when the person who offered him the deal was a close friend. Also, he knew there that the company had an excellent chance for growth; still he turned down the opportunity.

The station eventually made a whopping $73 million pre-tax. And since then, the value of the company was put at $800 million.

Finally, a lot can be learned from Buffett's success stories. However, a lot can also be learned from his losses and near misses. Each part had the role it played in making him the successful businessman he is today.

Chapter 5

Warren Buffett
The Philanthropist

A s of 2008, Warren Buffett was the richest man in the world. His fortune was placed at approximately $62 billion. However, in 2009, he was toppled from that position after giving away a lot of his wealth.

Despite being the third richest man in the world, he still manages to live a very simple life. His home in Nebraska is worth less than one percent of his wealth. This commitment to frugality is only matched by his commitment to giving.

At the moment, Buffett is regarded as one of the most generous individuals who exist. However, he did not start out being so generous. It is reported that his foray into philanthropy was at the insistence of his first wife, Susan.

He had always stated his firm belief in philanthropy and his intention to give away his wealth to charity. Thus, in June of 2006, he announced plans to give away 83% of his wealth to the Bill and Melinda Gates Foundation.

He pledged about 20 million class B shares of Berkshire Hathaway shares. When he made the pledge, the shares were worth about $37 billion. Thus, this effectively makes it one of the largest charitable donations in history. Warren Buffett is now ranked as one of the leaders of philanthropy world over.

The gift is supposed to be given over a period of years. It is supposed to take effect upon Buffett's death. Ultimately, all of Buffett's shares would be given away, in small gifts, ten years after his death and the settling of his estate.

The estate he intends leaving to the foundation consists of his own shares of stocks in Berkshire Hathaway. Also, there exists cash which his heirs are supposed to invest in index funds.

Buffett's donation has given him a significant stake in the Bill and Melinda Gates Foundation. He currently serves on the foundation's board. However, he maintains that he wouldn't be actively vested in the foundation's investments.

Warren Buffett has a burning desire to solve most of the global problems that exist today. This has pushed him to encourage others to tow the same line as him. He routinely reaches out to his peers - the wealthiest of the wealthy world over - to do a lot more for charity.

His actions are informed by a firm belief that the Bill and Melinda Gates Foundation actually addresses global problems. This is especially so in the areas of health care and education.

Much of the foundation's efforts are directed towards reaching the world's poor. The foundation provides grants to individuals who are working to achieve the alleviation of poverty. They also fund researches into diseases and developing vaccines for deadly diseases. All of these are values Buffett subscribes to, and believes it will be a good investment of his estate.

Buffett's donation to the Bill and Melinda Gates is a departure from a view he held earlier. He had earlier stated that his estate would pass to his foundation upon death. In fact, the bulk of his wife's estate had gone to his foundation at her death.

Buffett has reiterated that his children will not receive a significant part of his wealth. They would receive some amount of cash and some Hathaway stock. His intention is to give them just enough for them to be comfortable without becoming indolent.

Buffett's aim is for his children to imbibe the values he holds dear. This includes being active in philanthropy and giving to charity.

Other Works of Charity by Warren Buffett

Apart from his donations to the Bill and Melinda Gates Foundation, Warren Buffett has made other signification donations to charity.

In 2006, he auctioned off his car on eBay and gave it all to the Girls Inc foundation. In 2007, he presided over an auction that raised over $650,000 for the Glide Foundation.

Over the course of the years, later auctions raised between $1.7 to 3.5 million. The winners are usually rewarded with a dinner with Buffett at the Wollensky Steak house in New York. The restaurant donates $10,000 to the Glide foundation each year to be able to host the dinner.

On July 16, 2018, Berkshire Hathaway announced that Buffett has donated over $3.4 billion worth of stock to five charities. That was the single biggest donation by Buffett to date. He made the donations to the Bill and Melinda Gates

Foundation, his own foundation, and charities run by his children.

The charities run by his children include Susan Alive Buffett's Sherwood foundation. The Howard G. Buffett Foundation run by his son, Howard. Lastly, is the NoVo Foundation run by his other son, Peter Buffett.

Buffett is also supportive of his sister's foundation; the Letters Foundation and the Learning by Giving Foundation.

So far, Buffett has donated enough money to build 5 Apple 'spaceship' campuses. Apple Spaceship Campuses are valued at $5 billion each. What this means is that in his lifetime, Warren Buffett has given away more than $25 billion.

A study carried out by CNBC has listed Warren Buffett and Bill Gates as the most charitable billionaires alive. The survey calculated the giving habit of the top wealthiest persons in the world beginning in 2000.

Warren Buffett's Involvement with the Giving Pledge

On December 9, 2010, Warren Buffett, Bill Gates, and Mark Zuckerberg instituted the giving pledge. The pledge is to give away half of their wealth over time to charity. They also made the decision to involve others to do the same.

Plans for the pledge began in June of 2010 by Warren Buffett and Bill Gates. By August, the aggregate wealth garnered was around $125 million. By April of the following year, 69 persons had become signatories.

As of 2019, the pledge has over 187 signatories. A lot of the signatories are billionaires, and their pledges have amounted up to $365 billion.

The pledge does not state exactly how the funds would be spent. Furthermore, the agreement is not a legal obligation, and there is no compunction to donate. The pledge claims that it is really just a moral obligation that is encouraged. Following this, every individual or couple who pledges writes a letter on the pledge's website explaining their reasons for doing so.

Conclusion

Value Investing

There is no doubt that Warren Buffett has revolutionized the way investment is done in the world today. He introduced a model that is being used by investors today, and has proved effective time and again. His primary investment strategy is known as **value investing**.

This choice was largely influenced by his long apprenticeship to Benjamin Graham. Value investing looks at the underlying value of a company as opposed to the worth of its stock price.

Buffett believes that investors should only invest in companies that can hold their stocks forever. He is a large believer in sticking with a company and growing with it over time. This, perhaps, informs his heavy investment in just a handful of companies over the years.

Buffett teaches Value investors to look for stocks that are undervalued by the market. Also, an alternative route could be searching for stocks that are valued but not recognized by buyers. He believes that with these stocks, eventually, the efficient market hypothesis will kick in. That after a while, the market would eventually turn around to favor those formerly undervalued stocks.

Buffett's method is to look at the company as a whole. He chooses stocks based on their potentials for the company. His interests usually lie in acquiring ownership of these companies that are capable of generating long term gain.

Using several anecdotes and quotes, he has put together a comprehensive guide to investors. Some of the famous lines include: "Never lose money," "It is better to get a great company at a fair price than a fair company at a great price."

Of course, some of these rules have themselves been broken by Buffett. This goes to show that the most fundamental of the rules is to know what works for one.

Buffett also teaches that before one purchases stock in a company, the individual needs to check a few things off of his list. Firstly, he needs to confirm that the company has consistently performed well. One sure way of knowing that is by taking a look at the company's return in investment.

Furthermore, the individual has to confirm that the company has consistently avoided excess debt. He also admonishes that the number of years the company has been public should act as a guide. Typically, he teaches that one should invest in companies that have been public for at least ten years.

Buying Underperforming Companies

Buffett has shown, by example, that it is possible to purchase underperforming companies and make them profitable.

His first example was with his company, Berkshire Hathaway. Using his uncanny ability to sense good deals, and following strictly the rules he set for himself, he has somehow made Berkshire outperform competitors. It has also made him avoid huge losses.

Despite his age – he is 87 years old; Buffett is still making long term plans for his company. In 2014, he wrote a very detailed letter to his investors. In it, he laid out his thoughts for the company for the next 50 years.

He touched on every subject, from liquidity to investment bankers. He further stated that the rate of growth of Berkshire Hathaway might be unsustainable in the coming years.

Like earlier stated, Warren Buffett is one man who has revolutionized how investments are carried out the world over. His system provides a practical, down to earth approach that has no doubt worked.

This same attitude is seen in how he runs every other area of his life. He doesn't live in a large house, doesn't collect expensive artifacts and what not. His endorsement of value marketing may be criticized, but one cannot deny that it is efficacious.

Warren Buffett's Personal Life

A lot has been written about Warren Buffett and his investment policy. However, important to this investment policy is his belief in frugality and family.

Warren Buffett first tried to get his wife's attention using a ukulele. His wife Susan's boyfriend at the time played the instrument. Warren then bought the instrument and tried to compete for Susan's affections.

Eventually, the ploy with the ukulele did not work, but Buffett did succeed in getting Susan's attention. They eventually got married in 1952 and had three children, Susie, Howard, and Peter.

In 1977, the couple began living apart. They remained married until Susan's death in 2004. In 2006, on his 76th birthday, Warren Buffett married his longtime companion, Astrid Menks. She had lived with them even before Susan left.

This bit of history is rarely discussed when Buffett's history is examined.

Buffett's frugality is also legendary. As about 2006, his annual salary was about $100,000. This was little compared to what other executives of his cadre earned at that time.

He has continued to live in the house he bought as far back as 1958. The house, which is situated in his hometown of Omaha, was purchased for $31, 500. He, however, owns a $4 million house in Laguna Beach.

The only indulgence he has allowed himself is the private jet he purchased in 1989. Prior to that time, he had been vocal in his condemnation of extravagant purchases by

CEOs. He also had the habit of making use of only public transportation.

In December 2006, it was widely reported that Buffett does not carry a phone, nor make use of the internet. He was reported to drive his own car too – a Cadillac. In 2013, he had just one old Nokia flip phone and had sent out only one email his entire life.

Buffett is famous for his love of the game of bridge. He reportedly spends as much as twelve hours playing the game each week. Sometimes in the company of fellow fan, Bill Gates.

Warren Buffett partnered with the producer, Christopher Webber to release an animated series called Secret Millionaires Club. The series was intended to teach children healthy financial habits. It features Warren Buffett and his longtime friend, Charles Munger.

Warren Buffett grew up a Presbyterian. Over the years, he has come to identify as an agnostic.

In September of 2014, an article by Fast Company examined Warren Buffett's "avoid at all cost" practice. This was in a bid to gain an insight into his personal principles. Warren's advice is for people to create a list of 25 accomplishments they intend achieving in the next few years of their life. Then pick five of those really important ones and start with them.

His advice is to prioritize the five items over the initial long list. In fact, he is known to say "Avoid at all cost the longer list as they would impede the achievement of the top five."

Warren Buffett's life has served as an inspiration to a lot of investors all over the world. He often takes out time to speak at conferences, sharing his life experiences with up and coming investors. His speeches, while practical, are often laced with humor and personal anecdotes.

Buffett is known to draw inspiration from varied sources, including the bible and even Mae West. His is such a wide reach that his annual report to shareholders receives coverage by the media.

In fact, the Berkshire annual shareholders meeting in Omaha draws over 20,000 persons each year. Half of the population usually comprise of those seeking to learn from the acclaimed wizard of Wall Street.

Buffett's person has garnered such publicity that he has more books written about him than any other entrepreneur alive. In fact, in 2008, USA today reported that no less than 47 books are in print bearing Buffett's name. Those are not books written by him but books written about him, his investment style, and philosophies.

Those are merely attempts at preserving his wisdom for the coming generation. The CEO of Border Books commented on how remarkable that was. He stated that only US presidents and such figures as the Dalai Lama have achieved that feat.

Some of the books include: *Buffett, Making of an American Capitalist* by Roger Lowenstein; *The Warren Buffett Way* by Robert Hagstrom and, *Warren Buffett Speaks: Wit and Wisdom from the World's Greatest investor* by Janet Lowe.

In 2012, Buffett was diagnosed with stage 1 prostate cancer. He decided to go through the rounds of chemotherapy needed to take care of his illness. On September 15 of the same year, he announced that he had finished the rounds of chemo required.

Lessons from Warren Buffett's Life

What makes Warren Buffett's story truly remarkable is the place he occupies in the league of billionaires.

In a world where wealthy people are always flaunting their riches, where the rich develop morbidly exorbitant hobbies, taking cruises on the Nile and vacations on a whim. In that world of the ostentatious living, Warren Buffett is a breath of fresh air.

For over fifty years, Warren Buffett has lived in the same house and taken the same breakfast that costs less than $15. As a joke, he sometimes buys the same for his friends, Bill Gates. This is even when the combined wealth of both men is higher than the GDPs of many countries.

His frugality, even in the face of such abundance teaches us to appreciate what we have. His brilliance at business and investment teaches us that following rules work. The fact that he failed severally, made mistakes and didn't become a millionaire till fifty is a lesson in itself.

Buffett teaches us that it is never too late to start. That no matter how far we fall, we can always get back up.

We can also learn so much from his large heart and commitment to philanthropy. His foray into philanthropy began late in his life. However, since he began, it appears there is no stopping him.

Singlehandedly, Warren Buffett has donated more than 20% of his wealth to charity. He even plans to give more away at his death through the giving pledge.

Of course, for a lot of folks, his frugality may not endear him to them. Some others think he is an old man too set in his ways to change.

They may be right. He is, after all, an old man. What his critics cannot deny, however they try, is that his methods work. Time and again, he has defied naysayers and proven his doubters wrong with his track record.

That in itself is the motivation anyone needs.

Made in the USA
Monee, IL
18 November 2021